ISBN 978-1-334-03580-7
PIBN 10572487

This book is a reproduction of an important historical work. Forgotten Books uses state-of-the-art technology to digitally reconstruct the work, preserving the original format whilst repairing imperfections present in the aged copy. In rare cases, an imperfection in the original, such as a blemish or missing page, may be replicated in our edition. We do, however, repair the vast majority of imperfections successfully; any imperfections that remain are intentionally left to preserve the state of such historical works.

English
Français
Deutsche
Italiano
Español
Português

www.forgottenbooks.com

Mythology Photography **Fiction**
Fishing Christianity **Art** Cooking
Essays Buddhism Freemasonry
Medicine **Biology** Music **Ancient
Egypt** Evolution Carpentry Physics
Dance Geology **Mathematics** Fitness
Shakespeare **Folklore** Yoga Marketing
Confidence Immortality Biographies
Poetry **Psychology** Witchcraft
Electronics Chemistry History **Law**
Accounting **Philosophy** Anthropology
Alchemy Drama Quantum Mechanics
Atheism Sexual Health **Ancient History**
Entrepreneurship Languages Sport
Paleontology Needlework Islam
Metaphysics Investment Archaeology
Parenting Statistics Criminology
Motivational

THE METHOD OF ITS SOLUTION.

THE ANNUAL DISCOURSE DELIVERED AT THE SEVENTY-
THIRD ANNIVERSARY OF THE AMERICAN COLONIZA-
TION SOCIETY, IN THE CHURCH OF THE COVENANT,
WASHINGTON, D. C., JANUARY 19, 1890,

BY

EDWARD W. BLYDEN, LL. D.

PUBLISHED BY REQUEST.

WASHINGTON:
GIBSON BROS., PRINTERS AND BOOKBINDERS.
1890.

THE AFRICAN PROBLEM.

ACTS xvi, 9.

I AM seriously impressed with a sense of the responsibility of my position to-night. I stand in the presence of the representatives of that great organization which seems first of all the associations in this country to have distinctly recognized the hand of God in the history of the Negro race in America—to have caught something of the meaning of the Divine purpose in permitting their exile to and bondage in this land. I stand also in the presence of what, for the time being at least, must be considered the foremost congregation of the land—the religious home of the President of the United States. There are present, also, I learn, on this occasion, some of the statesmen and lawmakers of the land.

My position, then, is one of honor as well as of responsibility, and the message I have to deliver, I venture to think, concerns directly or indirectly the whole human race. I come from that ancient country, the home of one of the great original races, occupied by the descendants of one of the three sons to whom, according to Biblical history, the whole world was assigned—a country which is now engaging the active attention of all Europe. I come, also, from the ancestral home of at least five millions in this land. Two hundred millions of people have sent me on an errand of invitation to their blood relations here. Their cry is, "Come over and help us." And I find among hundreds of thousands of the invited an eager and enthusiastic response. They tell me to wave the answer across the deep to the anxious and expectant hearts, which, during the long and weary night of separation, have been constantly watching and praying for the return—to the Rachels weeping for their children, and refusing to be comforted because they are not—they tell me, "Wave the answer back to our brethren to hold the fort for we are coming." They have for the last seventy years been returning through the agency of the Society whose anniversary we celebrate to-night. Some have gone every year during that period, but they have been few compared to the vast necessity. They have gone as they have been able to go, and are making an impression for good upon that continent. My subject to-night will be, THE AFRICAN PROBLEM AND THE METHOD OF ITS SOLUTION.

This is no new problem. It is nearly as old as recorded history. It has interested thinking men in Europe and Asia in all ages. The imagination of the ancients peopled the interior of that country with a race of beings shut out from and needing no intercourse with the rest of mankind— lifted by their purity and simplicity of character above the necessity of intercourse with other mortals—leading a blameless and protracted existence and producing in their sequestered, beautiful, and fertile home, from which flowed the wonderful Nile, the food of the Gods. Not milk and honey but nectar and ambrosia were supposed to abound there. The Greeks especially had very high conceptions of the sanctity and spirituality of the interior Africans. The greatest of their poets picture the Gods as vacating Olympus every year and proceeding to Ethiopia to be feasted by its inhabitants. Indeed, the religion of some portion of Greece is supposed to have been introduced from Africa. But leaving the region of mythology, we know that the three highest religions known to mankind—if they had not their origin in Africa—were domiciled there in the days of their feeble beginnings, Judaism, Christianity, and Mohammedanism.

A sacred mystery hung over that continent, and many were the aspirations of philosophers and poets for some definite knowledge of what was beyond the narrow fringe they saw. Julius Cæsar, fascinated while listening to a tale of the Nile, lost the vision of military glory. The philosopher overcame the soldier and he declared himself ready to abandon for a time the alluring fields of politics in order to trace out the sources of that mysterious river which gave to mankind Egypt with her magnificent conceptions and splendid achievements.

The mystery still remains. The problem continues unsolved. The conquering races of the world stand perplexed and worried before the difficulties which beset their enterprise of reducing that continent to subjection. They have overcome the whole of the Western Hemisphere. From Behring Straits to Cape Horn America has submitted to their sway. The native races have almost disappeared from the mainland and the islands of the sea. Europe has extended her conquests to Australia, New Zealand, and the Archipelagos of the Pacific. But, for hundreds of years, their ships have passed by those tempting regions, where "Afric's sunny fountains roll down their golden sands," and though touching at different points on the coast, they have been able to acquire no extensive foothold in that country. Notwithstanding the reports we receive on every breeze that blows from the East, of vast " spheres of influence " and large European possessions, the points actually occupied by white men in the boundless equatorial regions of that immense continent may be accurately represented on the map only by microscopic dots. I wish that the announcements we receive from time to time with such a flourish of trumpets, that a genuine civilization is being carried into the heart of the Dark Continent, were true. But the fact is, that the bulk of Central Africa is being rapidly subjected to Mohammedanism. That system will soon be—or rather is now—knitting together the conquerors and the conquered into a harmonious whole ; and unless Europe gets a thorough understanding of the situation, the gates of missionary enterprise will be closed ; because, from all we can learn of the proceedings of some, especially in East Africa, the industrial *régime* is being stamped out to foster the militant. The current number of the *Fortnightly*, near the close of an interesting article on "Stanley's Expedition," has this striking sentence : "Stanley has triumphed, but Central Africa is darker than ever !"

It would appear that the world outside of Africa has not yet stopped to consider the peculiar conditions which lift that continent out of the range of the ordinary agencies by which Europe has been able to occupy other countries and subjugate or exterminate their inhabitants.

They have not stopped to ponder the providential lessons on this subject scattered through the pages of history, both past and contemporary.

First. Let us take the most obvious lesson as indicated in the climatic conditions. Perhaps in no country in the world is it so necessary (as in Africa) that the stranger or new comer should possess the *mens sana in corpore sano*— the sound mind in sound body; for the climate is most searching, bringing to the surface any and every latent physical or mental defect. If a man has any chronic or hereditary disease it is sure to be developed, and if wrong medical treatment is applied it is very apt to be exaggerated and often to prove fatal to the patient. And as with the body so with the mind. Persons of weak minds, either months on the Gold Coast or Lagos; and for every three days during which they are kept on the coast after the time for their leave arrives, they are allowed one day in Europe. The neglect of this regulation is often attended with most serious consequences.

Second. When we come into the moral and intellectual world it would seem as if the Almighty several times attempted to introduce the foreigner and a foreign civilization into Africa and then changed his purpose. The Scriptures seem to warrant the idea that in some way inexplicable to us, and incompatible with our conception of the character of the Sovereign of the Universe, the unchangeable Being sometimes reverses His apparent plans. We read that, "it repented God," &c. For thousands of years the northeastern portion of Africa witnessed a wonderful development of civilization. The arts and sciences flourished in Egypt for generations, and that country was the centre of almost universal influence; but there was no effect produced upon the interior of Africa. So North Africa became the seat of a great military and commercial power which flourished for 700 years. After this the Roman Catholic Church constructed a mighty influence in the same region, but the interior of the continent received no impression from it.

In the fifteenth century the Congo country, of which we now hear so much, was the scene of extensive operations of the Roman Catholic Church. Just a little before the discovery of America thousands of the natives of the Congo, including the most influential families, were baptized by Catholic missionaries; and the Portuguese, for a hundred years, devoted themselves to the work of African evangelization and exploration. It would appear that they knew just as much of interior Africa as is known now after the great exploits of Speke and Grant and Livingstone, Baker and Cameron and Stanley. It is said that there is a map in the Vatican, three hundred years old, which gives all the general physical relief and the river and lake systems of Africa with more or less accuracy; but the Arab geographers of a century before had described the mountain system, the great lakes, and the course of the Nile.

Just about the time that Portugal was on the way to establish a great empire on that continent, based upon the religious system of Rome, America was discovered, and, instead of the Congo, the Amazon became the seat of Portuguese power. Neither Egyptian, Carthaginian, Persian, or Roman influence was allowed to establish itself on that continent. It would seem that in the providential purpose no solution of the African problem was to come from alien sources. Africans were not doomed to share the fate of some other dark races who have come in contact with the aggressive European. Europe was diverted to the Western Hemisphere. The energies of that conquering race, it was decreed, should be spent in building up a home for themselves on this side. Africa followed in chains.

The Negro race was to be preserved for a special and important work in the future. Of the precise nature of that work no one can form any definite conception. It is probable that if foreign races had been allowed to enter their country they would have been destroyed. So they were brought over to be helpers in this country and at the same time to be preserved. It was not the first time in the history of the world that a people have been preserved by subjection to another people. We know that God promised Abraham that his seed should inherit the land of Canaan; but when He saw that in their numerically weak condition they would have been destroyed in conflicts with the indigenous inhabitants, he took them down to Egypt and kept them there in bondage four hundred years that they might be fitted, both by discipline and numerical increase, for the work that would devolve upon them. Slavery would seem to be a strange school in which to preserve a people; but God has a way of salting as well as purifying by fire.

The Europeans, who were fleeing from their own country in search of wider areas of freedom and larger scope for development, found here an aboriginal race unable to co-operate with them in the labors required for the construction of the material framework of the new civilization. The Indians would not work, and they have suffered the consequences of that indisposition. They have passed away. To take their place as accessories in the work to be done God suffered the African to be brought hither, who could work and would work, and could endure the climatic conditions of a new southern country, which Europeans could not. Two currents set across the Atlantic towards the west for nigh three hundred years—the one from Europe, the other from Africa. The one from Africa had a crimson color. From that stream of human beings millions fell victims to the cruelties of the middle passage, and otherwise suffered from the brutal instincts of their kidnappers and enslavers. I do not know whether Africa has been invited to the celebration of the fourth centenary of the discovery of America; but she has quite as much reason, if not as much right, to participate in the demonstration of that occasion as the European nations. 'Englishman, Hollander, and Huguenot, Nigritian and Congo came together. If Europe brought the head, Africa furnished the hands for a great portion of the work which has been achieved here, though it was the opinion of an African chief that the man who discovered America ought to have been imprisoned for having uncovered one people for destruction and opened a field for the oppression and suffering of another.

But when the new continent was opened Africa was closed. The veil, which was being drawn aside, was replaced, and darkness once more enveloped the land, for then not the *country* but the *people* were needed. They were to do a work elsewhere, and meanwhile their country was to be shut out from the view of the outside world.

The first Africans landed in this country in the State of Virginia in the year 1619. Then began the first phase of what is called the Negro problem. These people did not come hither of their own accord. Theirs was not a voluntary but a compulsory expatriation. The problem, then, on their arrival in this country, which confronted the white people was how to reduce to effective and profitable servitude an alien race which it was neither possible nor desirable to assimilate. This gave birth to that peculiar institution, established in a country whose *raison d'être* was that all men might enjoy the "right to life, liberty, and the pursuit of happiness." Laws had to be enacted by Puritans, Cavaliers, and Roundheads for slaves, and every contrivance had to be devised for the safety of the institution. It was a difficult problem, in the effort to solve which both master and slave suffered.

It would seem, however, that in the first years of African slavery in this country, the masters upon many of whom the relationship was forced, understood its providential origin and purpose, until after a while, avarice and greed darkened their perceptions, and they began to invent reasons, drawn even from the Word of God, to justify their holding these people in perpetual bondage for the advantage of themselves and their children forever. But even after a blinding cupidity had captured the generality by its bewitching spell, there were those (far-sighted men, especially after the yoke of Great Britain had been thrown off) who saw that the abnormal relation could not be permanent under the democratic conditions established by the fundamental law of the land. It was Thomas Jefferson, the writer of the Declaration of Independence, who made the celebrated utterance : " Nothing is more clearly written in the Book of Destiny than the emancipation of the blacks ; and it is equally certain that the two races will never live in a state of equal freedom under the same Government, so insurmountable are the barriers which nature, habit, and opinion have established between them."

For many years, especially in the long and weary period of the anti-slavery conflict, the latter part of this dictum of Jefferson was denounced by many good and earnest men. The most intelligent of the colored people resented it as a prejudiced and anti-Christian conception. But as the years go by and the Negroes rise in education and culture, and therefore in love and pride of race, and in proper conception of race gifts, race work and race destiny, the latter clause of that famous sentence is not only being shorn of its obscurity and repulsiveness, but is being welcomed as embodying a truth indispensable to the pres- ervation and prosperity of both races, and as pointing to the regeneration of the African Fatherland. There are some others of the race who, recognizing Jefferson's prin- ciple, would make the races one by amalgamation.

It was under the conviction of the truth expressed by that statesman that certain gentlemen of all political shades and differing religious views, met together in this city in the winter of 1816–'17, and organized the American Colonization Society. Though friendly to the anti-slavery idea, and anxious for the extinction of the abnormal in- stitution, these men did not make their views on that sub- jcet prominent in their published utterances. They were not Abolitionists in the political or technical sense of that phrase. But their labors furnished an outlet and en- couragement for persons desiring to free their slaves, giv- ing them the assurance that their freedmen would be re- turned to their Fatherland, carrying thither what light of Christianity and civilization they had received. It seems a pity that this humane, philanthropic, and far- seeing work should have met with organized opposition from another band of philanthropists, who, anxious for a speedy deliverance of the captives, thought they saw in the Colonization Society an agency for riveting instead of breaking the fetters of the slave, and they denounced it with all the earnestness and eloquence they could com- mand, and they commanded, both among whites and blacks, some of the finest orators the country has ever produced. And they did a grand work, both directly and indirectly, for the Negro and for Africa. They did their work and dissolved their organization. But when their work was done the work of the Colonization Society really began.

In the development of the Negro question in this country the colonizationists might be called the prophets and philosophers; the abolitionists, the warriors and politicians. Colonizationists saw what was coming and patiently prepared for its advent. Abolitionists attacked the first phase of the Negro problem and labored for its immediate solution; colonizationists looked to the last phase of the problem and labored to get both the whites and blacks ready for it. They labored on two continents, in America and in Africa. Had they not begun as early as they did to take up lands in Africa for the exiles, had they waited for the abolition of slavery, it would now have been impossible to obtain a foothold in their fatherland for the returning hosts. The colonizationist, as prophet, looked at the State as it would be ; the abolitionist, as politician, looked at the State as it was. The politician sees the present and is possessed by it. The prophet sees the future and gathers inspiration from it. The politician may influence legislation ; the prophet, although exercising great moral influence, seldom has any legislative power. The agitation of the politician may soon culminate in legal enactments ; the teachings of the prophet may require generations before they find embodiment in action. The politician has to-day ; the prophet, to-morrow. The politician deals with facts, the prophet with ideas, and ideas take root very slowly. Though nearly three generations have passed away since Jefferson made his utterance, and more than two since the organization of the Colonization Society, yet the conceptions they put forward can scarcely be said to have gained maturity, much less currency, in the public mind. But the recent discussions in the halls of Congress show that the teachings of the prophet are now beginning to take hold of the politician. It may take many years yet before the people come up to these views, and, therefore, before legislation upon them may be possible, but there is evidently movement in that direction.

The first phase of the Negro problem was solved at Appomattox, after the battle of the warrior, with confused noise and garments rolled in blood. The institution of slavery, for which so many sacrifices had been made, so many of the principles of humanity had been violated, so many of the finer sentiments of the heart had been stifled, was at last destroyed by violence.

Now the nation confronts the second phase, the educational, and millions are being poured out by State governments and by individual philanthropy for the education of the freedmen, preparing them for the third and last phase of the problem, viz : EMIGRATION.

In this second phase, we have that organization, which might be called the successor of the old Anti-Slavery Society, taking most active and effective part. I mean the American Missionary Association. I have watched with constant gratitude and admiration the course and operations of that Society, especially when I remember that, organized in the dark days of slavery, twenty years before emancipation, it held aloft courageously the banner on which was inscribed freedom for the Negro and no fellowship with his oppressors. And they, among the first, went South to lift the freedmen from the mental thraldom and moral degradation in which slavery had left him. They triumphed largely over the spirit of their opponents. They braved the dislike, the contempt, the apprehension with which their work was at first regarded, until they succeeded by demonstrating the advantages of knowledge over ignorance, to bring about that state of things to which Mr. Henry Grady, in his last utterances, was able to refer with such satisfaction, viz., that since the war the South has spent $122,000,000 in the cause of public education, and this year it is pledged to spend $37,000,000, in the benefits of which the Negro is a large participant.

It is not surprising that some of those who, after having been engaged in the noble labors of solving the first phase of the problem—in the great anti-slavery war—and are now confronting the second phase, should be unable to receive with patience the suggestion of the third, which is the emigration phase, when the Negro, freed in body and in mind, shall bid farewell to these scenes of his bondage and discipline and betake himself to the land of his fathers, the scene of larger opportunities and loftier achievements. I say it is not surprising that the veterans of the past and the present should be unable to give much enthusiasm to the work of the future. It is not often given to man to labor successfully in the land of Egypt, in the wilderness and across the Jordan. Some of the most effective workers, must often, with eyes undimmed and natural force unabated, lie down and die on the borders of full freedom, and if they live, life to them is like a dream. The young must take up the work. To old men the indications of the future are like a dream. Old men are like them that dream. Young men see visions. They catch the spirit of the future and are able to place themselves in accord with it.

But things are not yet ready for the solution of the third and last phase of the problem. Things are not ready in this country among whites or blacks. The industrial condition of the South is not prepared for it. Things are not yet ready in Africa for a complete exodus. Europe is not yet ready; she still thinks that she can take and utilize Africa for her own purposes. She does not yet understand that Africa is to be for the African or for nobody. Therefore she is taking up with renewed vigor, and confronting again, with determination, the

African problem. Englishmen, Germans, Italians, Belgians, are taking up territory and trying to wring from the grey-haired mother of civilization the secret of the ages. Nothing has come down from Egypt so grand and impressive as the Sphinxes that look at you with calm and emotionless faces, guarding their secret to-day as they formerly guarded the holy temples. They are a symbol of Africa. She will not be forced. She only can reveal her secret. Her children trained in the house of bondage will show it to the world. Some have already returned and have constructed an independent nation as a beginning of this work on her western borders.

It is a significant fact that Africa was completely shut up until the time arrived for the emancipation of her children in the Western World. When Jefferson and Washington and Hamilton and Patrick Henry were predicting and urging the freedom of the slave, Mungo Park was beginning that series of explorations by English enterprise which has just ended in the expedition of Stanley. Just about the time that England proclaimed freedom throughout her colonies, the brothers Lander made the great discovery of the mouth of the Niger ; and when Lincoln issued the immortal proclamation, Livingstone was unfolding to the world that wonderful region which Stanley has more fully revealed and which is becoming now the scene of the secular and religious activities of Christendom. The King of the Belgians has expended fortunes recently in opening the Congo and in introducing the appliances of civilization, and by a singular coincidence a bill has been brought forward in the U. S. Senate to assist the emigration of Negroes to the Fatherland just at the time when that philanthropic monarch has despatched an agent to this country to invite the co-operation in his great work of qualified freedmen. This is significant.

have exhausted themselves in costly experiments to utilize white men as colonists in Africa. They will then understand the purpose of the Almighty in having permitted the exile and bondage of the Africans, and they will see that for Africa's redemption the Negro is the chosen instrument. They will encourage the establishment and building up of such States as Liberia. They will recognize the scheme of the Colonization Society as the providential one.

The little nation which has grown up on that coast as a result of the efforts of this Society, is now taking hold upon that continent in a manner which, owing to inexperience, it could not do in the past. The Liberians have introduced a new article into the commerce of the world—the Liberian coffee. They are pushing to the interior, clearing up the forests, extending the culture of coffee, sugar, cocoa, and other tropical articles, and are training the aborigines in the arts of civilization and in the principles of Christianity. The Republic occupies five hundred miles of coast with an elastic interior. It has a growing commerce with various countries of Europe and America. No one who has visited that country and has seen the farms on the banks of the rivers and in the interior, the workshops, the schools, the churches, and other elements and instruments of progress will say that the United States, through Liberia, is not making a wholesome impression upon Africa—an impression which, if the members of the American Congress understood, they would not begrudge the money required to assist a few hundred thousand to carry on in that country the work so well begun. They would gladly spare them from the laboring element of this great nation to push forward the enterprises of civilization in their Fatherland, and to build themselves up on the basis of their race manhood.

If there is an intelligent Negro here to-night I will say to him, let me take you with me in imagination to witness the new creation or development on that distant shore ; I will not paint you an imaginary picture, but will describe an historical fact; I will tell you of reality. Going from the coast, through those depressing alluvial plains which fringe the eastern and western borders of the continent, you reach, after a few miles' travel, the first high or undulating country, which, rising abruptly from the swamps, enchants you with its solidity, its fertility, its verdure, its refreshing and healthful breezes. You go further, and you stand upon a higher elevation where the wind sings more freshly in your ears, and your heart beats fast as you survey the continuous and unbroken forests that stretch away from your feet to the distant horizon. The melancholy cooing of the pigeons in some unseen retreat or the more entrancing music of livelier and picturesque songsters alone disturb the solemn and almost oppressive solitude. You hear no human sound and see the traces of no human presence. You decline to pursue your adventurous journey. You refuse to penetrate the lonely forest that confronts you. You return to the coast, thinking of the long ages which have elapsed, the seasons which, in their onward course, have come and gone, leaving those solitudes undisturbed. You wonder when and how are those vast wildernesses to be made the scene of human activity and to contribute to human wants and happiness. Finding no answer to your perplexing question you drop the subject from your thoughts. After a few years—a very few it may be— you return to those scenes. To your surprise and gratification your progress is no longer interrupted by the inconvenience of bridle-paths and tangled vines. The roads are open and clear. You miss the troublesome creeks and drains which, on your previous journey,

harassed and fatigued you. Bridges have been constructed, and without any of the former weariness you find
yourself again on the summit, where in loneliness you had
stood sometime before. What do you now see? The
gigantic trees have disappeared, houses have sprung up
on every side. As far as the eye can see the roofs of com-
fortable and homelike cottages peep through the wood.
The waving corn and rice and sugar-cane, the graceful and
fragrant coffee tree, the umbrageous cocoa, orange, and
mango plum have taken the place of the former sturdy
denizens of the forest. What has brought about the
change? The Negro emigrant has arrived from America,
and, slender though his facilities have been, has produced
these wonderful revolutions. You look beyond and take
in the forests that now appear on the distant horizon.
You catch glimpses of native villages embowered in plan-
tain trees, and you say these also shall be brought under
civilized influences, and you feel yourself lifted into manhood, the spirit of the teacher and guide and missionary
comes upon you, and you say, "There, below me and beyond lies the world into which I must go. There must I
cast my lot. I feel I have a message to it, or a work in
it;" and the sense that there are thousands dwelling there,
some of whom you may touch, some of whom you may influence, some of whom may love you or be loved by you,
thrills you with a strange joy and expectation, and it is a
thrill which you can never forget; for ever and anon it comes
upon you with increased intensity. In that hour you are
born again. You hear forevermore the call ringing in
your ears, " Come over and help us."

These are the visions that rise before the Liberian set-
tler who has turned away from the coast. This is the view
that exercises such an influence upon his imagination, and
gives such tone to his character, making him an inde-

pendent and productive man on the continent of his fathers.

As I have said, this is no imaginary picture, but the embodiment of sober history. Liberia, then, is a fact, an aggressive and progressive fact, with a great deal in its past and everything in its future that is inspiring and uplifting.

It occupies one of the most charming countries in the western portion of that continent. It has been called by qualified judges the garden spot of West Africa. I love to dwell upon the memories of scenes which I have passed through in the interior of that land. I have read of countries which I have not visited—the grandeur of the Rocky Mountains and the charms of the Yosemite Valley, and my imagination adds to the written description and becomes a gallery of delightful pictures. But of African scenes my memory is a treasure-house in which I delight to revel. I have distinctly before me the days and dates when I came into contact with their inexhaustible beauties. Leaving the coast line, the seat of malaria, and where are often seen the remains of the slaver's barracoons, which always give an impression of the deepest melancholy, I come to the high table-lands with their mountain scenery and lovely valleys, their meadow streams and mountain rivulets, and there amid the glories of a changeless and unchanging nature, I have taken off my shoes and on that consecrated ground adored the God and Father of the Africans.

This is the country and this is the work to which the American Negro is invited. This is the opening for him which, through the labors of the American Colonization Society, has been effected. This organization is more than a *colonization* society, more than an emigration society. It might with equal propriety and perhaps with greater accuracy be called the African *Repatriation* Society; or since the idea of planting towns and introducing extensive cultivation of the soil is included in its work, it might be called the African Repatriation and Colonization Society, for then you bring in a somewhat 'higher idea than mere colonization—the mere settling of a new country by strangers—you bring in the idea of restoration, of compensation to a race and country much and long wronged.

Colonizationists, notwithstanding all that has been said against them, have always recognized the manhood of the Negro and been willing to trust him to take care of himself. They have always recognized the inscrutable providence by which the African was brought to these shores. They have always taught that he was brought hither to be trained out of his sense of irresponsibility to a knowledge of his place as a factor in the great work of humanity ; and that after having been thus trained he could find his proper sphere of action only in the land of his origin to make a way for himself. They have believed that it has not been given to the white man to fix the intellectual or spiritual status of this race. They have recognized that the universe is wide enough and God's gifts are varied enough to allow the man of Africa to find out a path of his own within the circle of genuine human interests, and to contribute from the field of his particular enterprise to the resources—material, intellectual, and moral—of the great human family.

But will the Negro go to do this work ?

Is he willing to separate himself from a settled civilization which he has helped to build up to betake himself to the wilderness of his ancestral home and begin anew a career on his own responsibility ?

I believe that he is. And if suitable provision were made for their departure to-morrow hundreds of thousands would avail themselves of it. The African question, or the because the pressure of commercial and political exigencies does not allow time and leisure to the stronger and richer elements of the nation to study it. It is not a question of color simply—that is a superficial accident. It lies deeper than color. It is a question of race, which is the outcome not only of climate, but of generations subjected to environments which have formed the mental and moral constitution.

It is a question in which two distinct races are concerned. This is not a question then purely of reason. It is a question also of instinct. Races feel; observers theorize.

The work to be done beyond the seas is not to be a reproduction of what we see in this country. It requires, therefore, distinct race perception and entire race devotion. It is not to be the healing up of an old sore, but the unfolding of a new bud, an evolution; the development of a new side of God's character and a new phase of humanity. God said to Moses, "I am that I am;" or, more exactly, "I shall be that I shall be." Each race sees from its own standpoint a different side of the Almighty. The Hebrews could not see or serve God in the land of the Egyptians; no more can the Negro under the Anglo-Saxon. He can serve *man* here. He can furnish the labor of the country, but to the inspiration of the country he must ever be an alien.

In that wonderful sermon of St. Paul on Mars Hill in which he declared that God hath made of one blood all nations of men to dwell on all the face of the earth and hath determined the bounds of their habitation, he also said, "In Him we live and move and have our being."

Now it cannot be supposed that in the types and races which have already displayed themselves God has exhansted himself. It is by God in **us**, where we have freedom to act out ourselves, that we do each our several work and live out into action, through our work, whatever we have within us of noble and wise and true. What we do is, if we are able to be true to our nature, the **representation** of some phase of the Infinite Being. If we live and move and have our being in Him, God also lives, and moves and has His being in us. This is why slavery of any kind is an outrage. It spoils the image of God as it strives to express itself through the individual or the race. As in the Kingdom of Nature, we see in her great organic types of being, in the movement, changes, and order of the elements, those vast thoughts of God, so in the great types of man, in the various races of the world, as distinct in character as in work, in the great divisions of character, we see the will and character and consciousness of God disclosed to us. According to this truth a distinct phase of God's character is set forth to be wrought out into perfection in every separate character. As in every form of the inorganic universe we see some noble variation of God's thought and beauty, so in each separate man, in each separate race, something of the absolute is incarnated. The whole of mankind is a vast representation of the Deity. Therefore we cannot extinguish any race either by conflict or amalgamation without serious responsibility.

You can easily see then why one race overshadowed by another should long to express itself—should yearn for the opportunity to let out the divinity that stirs within it. This is why the Hebrews cried to God from the depths of their affliction in Egypt, and this is why thousands and thousands of Negroes in the South are longing to go to the land of their fathers. They are not content to remain where everything has been done on the line of another race. They long for the scenes where everything is to be done under the influence of a new racial spirit, under the impulse of new skies and the inspiration of a fresh development. Only those are fit for this new work who believe in the race—have faith in its future—a prophetic insight into its destiny from a consciousness of its possibilities. The inspiration of the race is in the race.

Only one race has furnished the prophets for humanity—the Hebrew race; and before they were qualified to do this they had to go down to the depths of servile degradation. Only to them were revealed those broad and pregnant principles upon which every race can stand and work and grow; but for the special work of each race the prophets arise among the people themselves.

What is pathetic about the situation is, that numbers among whites and blacks are disposed to ignore the seriousness and importance of the question. They seem to think it a question for political manipulation and to be dealt with by partisan statesmanship, not recognizing the fact that the whole country is concerned. I freely admit the fact, to which attention has been recently called, that there are many Afro-Americans who have no more to do with Africa than with Iceland, but this does not destroy the truth that there are millions whose life is bound up with that continent. It is to them that the message comes from their brethren across the deep, "Come over and help us."

CPSIA information can be obtained
at www.ICGtesting.com
Printed in the USA
BVHW04s0417150818
524535BV00009B/91/P